ICE CREAM DREAMS

A&B Publishers Group
Brooklyn, New York
11238

Ice Cream Dreams © 2001 By Brittney Moniqué Grimes. All rights reserved. No part of this book may be reproduced in any form or by any means including electronic, mechanical or photocopying or stored in a retrieval system without permission in writing from the publisher except by a reviewer who may quote brief passage to be included in a review.

Published
by

A&B PUBLISHERS GROUP
1000 Atlantic Avenue
Brooklyn, New York,
11238

All poems written by Brittney Grimes
All artwork and illustrations on the following pages
23, 26, 27, 28, 29, 30, 33, 39, 48, 49, 50, 51, 54, 55, 58, 61, 71, by Brittney Grimes.

first edition

ISBN 1-886433-83-6 (paper)
ISBN 1-886433-84-4 (cloth)

10   9   8   7   6   5   4   3   2   1

Manufactured and Printed in the United States

ICE CREAM DREAMS

A book of poems
written and illustrated
by

BRITTNEY MONIQUÉ GRIMES

DEDICATION

To my Dear Grand-dad

Mr. Alfonzo Grimes Sr.
1926-2000

He will live forever in my heart!

Grand-dad

Even though I've known you a short period of time,
there is one thing I know for sure!
You were a caring and sweet grandad
with a heart so kind and pure.

I am sad that you passed on,
leaving bowed heads and eyes full of tears.
I am happy to have had a grandad so loving
and kind to so many people through the years.

I am sad that you are gone and happy that
you are with God and Jesus above.
You're in a better place with no suffering, no pain
and a place filled with peace and love!

ABOUT THE BOOK

Brittney has sprinkled the pages of *Ice Cream Dreams* with precious pearls of wisdom. Her insightful rhymes allow the reader to view the world through the eyes of a gifted child-poet. Colors, stars, clouds and emotions take on new dimensions as she uses her pen and brush to illuminate what we often take for granted. A great gift for a child, especially the child who aspires to write.

ALPHABETICAL LISTING

Page No.

A Better Day	25
A Special Pond	46
A very Special Person	13
Amazing Raindrops	50
Amazing Sun	70
Anything is Possible	63
At The Beach	31
Avocado	51
Bingo	49
Books, Books, Books	52
Chicken	61
Church Bells	29
Clouds	41
Colors	53
Cookies and tea	62
Created by God	8
Different	32
Earth	33
Father	12
Food For The Mind	38
God Almighty	9
God's Creations	18
Godmother	17
Grandparents	16
Guardian Angel	10
Hope	69
Ice Cream Dreams	23
Koala	72
Koalas	71
Lady Liberty	56
Manners	42
Mom and Dad	15
Morning Passes	44
Mother Bird	59
My Piano Star	30
My Secret Hiding Place	68

Page No.

Neptune	24
Peace, Joy and Love	21
Real True Friends	22
Safe	36
School Supplies	73
Shining Rainbow	37
Sister's Love	15
Smiley Town	54
Squirrel	55
Starfish	58
Stores	35
Suddenly I Turned Around	45
Teddy	65
Teeth	39
The Café	74
The Dream	20
The Gardener's Prayer	27
The Gift	78
The Girl Who Loved To Read	76
The Marching Soldiers	64
The Messy Room	47
The Mirror	26
The Rock	57
The Shining Candle	28
The Very Berry House	34
Things Come and Go	66
Thunder and Lightning	77
Time	40
Turkey	75
Violin	48
We're Different	67
What Mother's Day Means to Me	11
Wouldn't It be Great If	60
You and me	19
Your Neighbor	43

Ice Cream Dreams

CONTENTS

Title	Page No.
Created by God	8
God Almighty	9
Guardian Angel	10
What Mother's Day Means to Me	11
Father	12
A very Special Person	13
Mom and Dad	14
Sister's Love	15
Grandparents	16
Godmother	17
God's Creations	18
You and me	19
The Dream	20
Peace, Joy and Love	21
Real True Friends	22
Ice Cream Dreams	23
Neptune	24
A Better Day	25
The Mirror	26
The Gardener's Prayer	27
The Shining Candle	28
Church Bells	29
My Piano Star	30
At The Beach	31
Different	32
Earth	33
The Very Berry House	34
Stores	35
Safe	36
Shining Rainbow	37
Food For The Mind	38
Teeth	39
Time	40
Clouds	41
Manners	42
Your Neighbor	43
Morning Passes	44
Suddenly I Turned Around	45
A Special Pond	46
The Messy Room	47
Violin	48
Bingo	49
Amazing Raindrops	50
Avocado	51
Books, Books, Books	52
Colors	53
Smiley Town	54
Squirrel	55
Lady Liberty	56
The Rock	57
Starfish	58
Mother Bird	59
Wouldn't It be Great If	60
Chicken	61
Cookies and tea	62
Anything is Possible	63
The Marching Soldiers	64
Teddy	65
Things Come and Go	66
We're Different	67
My Secret Hiding Place	68
Hope	69
Amazing Sun	70
Koalas	71
Koala	72
School Supplies	73
The Cafe	74
Turkey	75
The Girl Who Loved To Read	76
Thunder and Lightning	77
The Gift	78

Ice Cream Dreams

Created by GOD

There is a God who created the Earth, moon, stars and light.

God also created morning, afternoon, evening and night.

He created the Heavens, as well as the flowing blue sea,

God became pretty lonely, so He created you and me.

God made the mountains high and the oceans very deep.

God gave the world to all of us, a special gift to keep.

GOD ALMIGHTY

God is the beginning,

God is the end.

I can trust God because,

He's my best friend.

I love God, He's my power

He protects me, hour after hour.

I will always follow God,

but evil tries to get in.

Whatever evil tries to do,

I will never let it win!

"Guardian Angel"

I believe angels are around us, here and there,
they always surround us.
They make sure we're alright.
They watch us during the day,
and when we sleep at night.

What Mother's Day Means To Me

Mother's Day is special,

Mother's Day means love,

Mother's Day means a lot to me,

Because my mother's an angel from above.

She came here from heaven by God's command

She's always there to listen and offer a helping hand.

No matter where life leads me, I have to be prepared!

My mother will always be part of me

and that's why I'm not scared!

Mother's Day is a special day that is set aside,

to show I care and love her dearly!

She'll always be my guide!

Happy Mother's Day

Ice Cream Dreams

Father

F - is for a **f**ather, who's love means more than any treasure

A - is for **a**ll your love you give, it can never be measured

T - is for a **t**errific dad that you are day after day

H - is for the **h**umble person you are in your own special way

E - is for **e**xtraordinary, gift from above

R - is for your **r**are, caring and special love

Some people think FATHER is just a word.

To me, it means a whole lot more!

A Very Special Person

Your voice is as peaceful as a dove,

It would be hard to live without your tender love.

You make me happy when I am feeling down.

You know how to put a smile on my face whenever there's a frown.

Whenever I need encouragement or someone to keep me calm,

You're a very special person to me and a terrific mom!

Mom

Mom and Dad

The air I breathe, trees outside,
    the mountain's peak, the ocean's tide.
The grass that is dressed in dew,
    the sky that is painted blue!
All of these things make me glad,
    but nothings as special
            as my mom and dad!

Sister's Love

I love trying different foods
and I love being in happy moods,
I love admiring a beautiful dove,
but nothing is as special
      As my sister's love!

Ice Cream Dreams

Grandparents

I love the smell of a flower,
    the rain falling when there's a shower.
I like watching the clouds float by
    in the beautiful blue sky.
When snowflakes gently touch me,
it makes me feel glad,
But nothing is more precious
        than my grandma and granddad.

Godmother

G- is for the great **G**odmother you are to me

O- is for **o**utstanding and you're as wonderful as can be

D- is for every **d**ay I think about you

M- is for the **m**arvelous things you say and do

O- is for the **o**verjoyed feeling I get when I see you

T- is for the **t**hings both of us love to do

H- is for your kind, caring and loving **h**eart

E- is for the **e**xcellent, Godmother you've been from the start

R- is for the **r**eason, I really want you to know,

    you're very special to me and I love you so!

Ice Cream Dreams

God's Creation

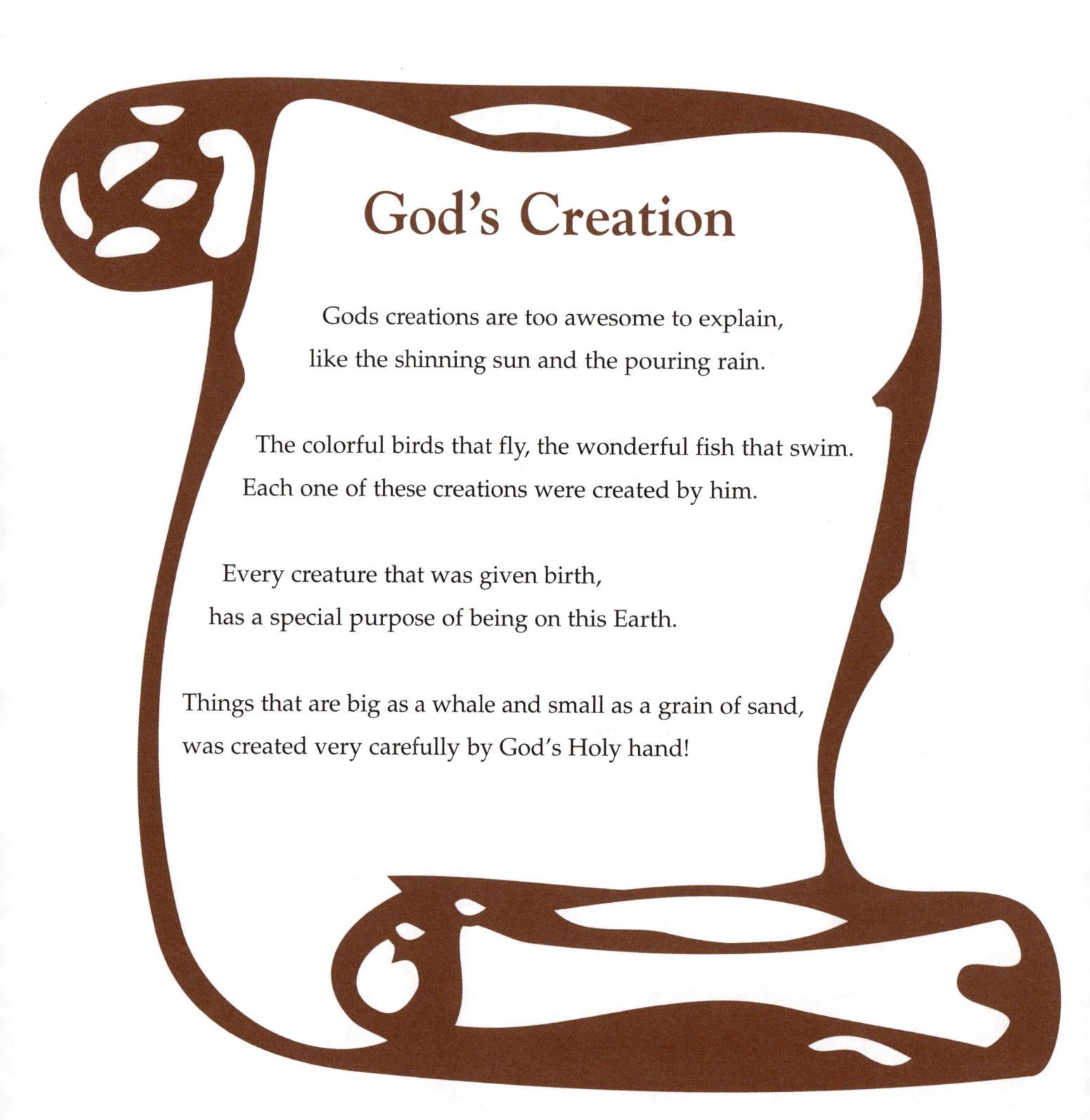

Gods creations are too awesome to explain,
like the shinning sun and the pouring rain.

The colorful birds that fly, the wonderful fish that swim.
Each one of these creations were created by him.

Every creature that was given birth,
has a special purpose of being on this Earth.

Things that are big as a whale and small as a grain of sand,
was created very carefully by God's Holy hand!

Ice Cream Dreams

You and Me

The petals on a flower, the leaves on a tree,

These are all gifts God gave to you and me.

The mighty roaring ocean, the flowing blue sea,

These are all gifts God gave to you and me.

Moms, dads and entire families,

These are special gifts God gave to you and me.

Ice Cream Dreams

The Dream

On August 28, 1963, Dr. King gave a great speech in Washington D.C.

It was a powerful speech, where he talked about equal rights.

He spoke to all people, Black, Red, Yellow and White.

Dr. Martin Luther King, Jr., had a dream that children of all colors,

would be able to join hands.

He wanted us to treat one another like brothers and sisters,

throughout this great land.

On August 28, 1989, "I" Brittney was born,

I too have a dream, that will help Dr. King's powerful message live on!

Peace, Joy and Love

Peace, joy and love

are three precious gifts from above.

Peace is when there are no more cries.

    Wouldn't it be wonderful if everyone had peace in their lives.

Joy is a feeling that's deep inside,

    it's a feeling of happiness, You just can't hide!

Love is a feeling we should show each other

    God never stops loving us, and we should love one another.

Real True Friends

Real friends are those
   who are kind and nice.
Real friends are helpful
   and give good advice.
Real friends help you up,
   when you've fallen down.
Real friends will lend a smile
   when you have a frown.

Real friends will help you understand,
   and will offer you a helping hand.
A real friend will try to help you
   when you have the flu,
or just make you feel better
   when you're feeling blue.
Real friends will help you bury your pet
   when it passes away.

Real friends pat you on your back
   and tell you, everything's O.K.
Now! let me question you,
Do you think your friend is true?

                               Be real!

Ice Cream Dreams

One night I had a dream that I always ate French Vanilla ice cream.
I ate French Vanilla ice cream every single day.
Whenever I was full, I ate it anyway.

I know it wasn't right, to eat ice cream every day and every night.
Girls and boys just remember this was just a dream.
It wouldn't be healthy if I ate that much ice cream.

Have an ice cream dream of your own!

Neptune

Neptune is the eighth planet from the sun.
Neptune has eight moons, Triton is the largest one.
Neptune has three rings that are faint and thin.
It takes Neptune 18 hours to make one complete spin.
"the Great Dark Spot" is a huge hurricane that never ends.
Neptune also has extremely cold and violent winds.
Methane is one of the gases that make Neptune look blue,
However, Neptune is made up of hydrogen and helium too.

A Better Day

Whenever I am lonely

Whenever I am scared

Whenever the world comes down on me and I am unprepared,

I fall on my knees and start to pray.

The Lords say to me "tomorrow's a better day!"

MIRROR

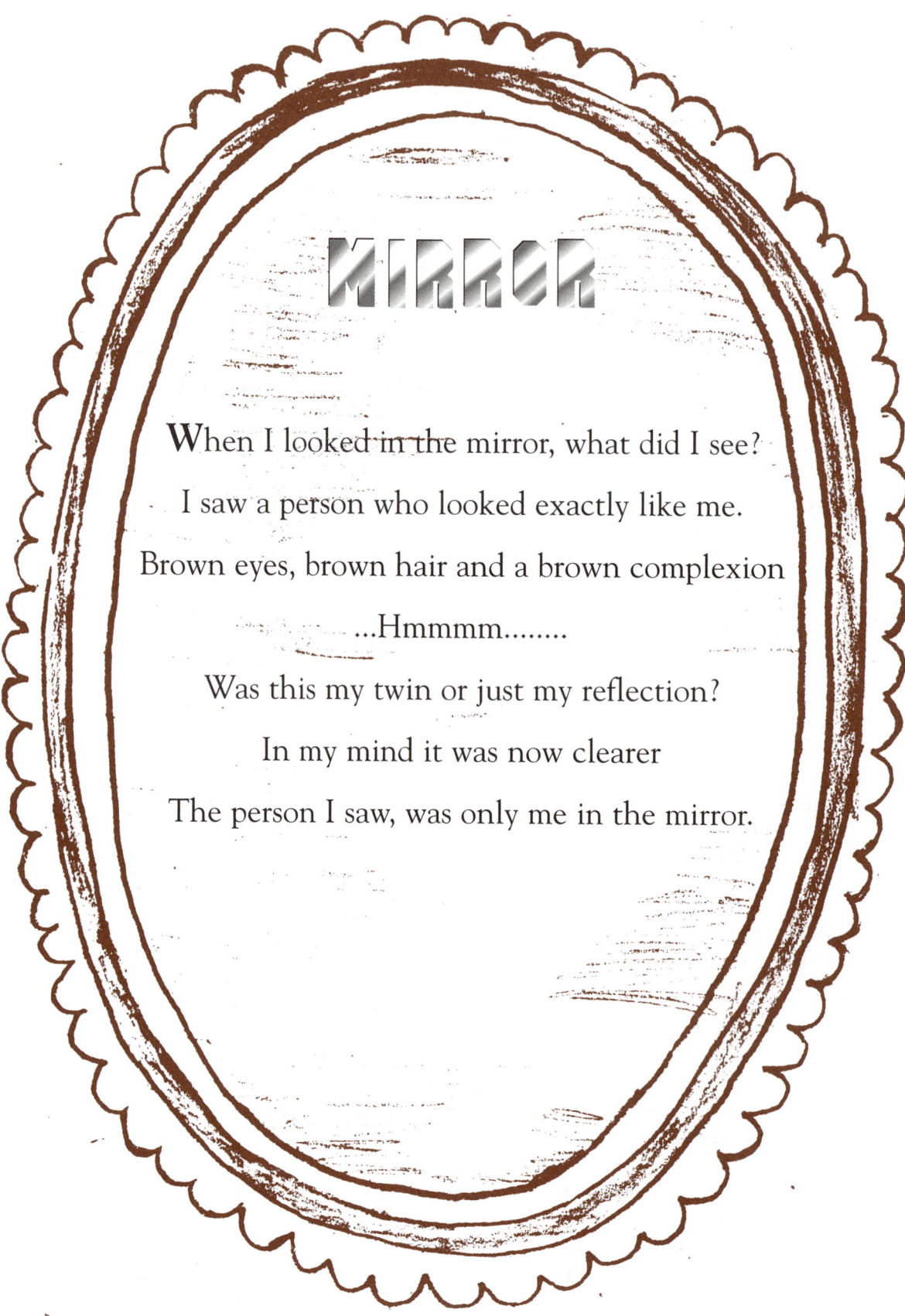

When I looked in the mirror, what did I see?

I saw a person who looked exactly like me.

Brown eyes, brown hair and a brown complexion

...Hmmmm........

Was this my twin or just my reflection?

In my mind it was now clearer

The person I saw, was only me in the mirror.

The Gardener's Prayer

Dear Lord,

Please bless this garden, my mom and I planted together.

Please help the flowers, sprout in all types of weather.

Please bless the flowers in winter, spring, summer and fall.

Please bless the flowers, blossoms, leaves, roots and all.

Please Lord with your love, help our little garden grow.

Help the flowers when the burning sun shines,

and when the rough winds blow.

Ice Cream Dreams

The Shining Candle

I once possessed a little candle,
which shined very bright
I loved its shiny purple handle
and its comforting light.
The candle's flame was yellow,
blue, orange and red.
The flame would light up my entire room
and make shadows over my bed.

Ice Cream Dreams

Church Bells

On a Sunday morning, church bells are ringing.

All of the people in the church pews are singing.

The people bow their heads to God and pray.

They give thanks to the Lord for giving then another day.

My Piano Star

This is an instrument that's fun to play,

To learn all the notes, you should practice everyday.

My sister is good and she plays more than one song.

I love to hear her play and I love to sing along.

At The Beach

People playing games, people having fun.
People getting suntans under the crisp hot sun.

People swimming in the water, while others play on land,
I also see children building castles out of golden sand.

Tiny pieces of sand, that is warmed by the sun's heat,
Is snuggled between little toes that cling to their feet.

Ice Cream Dreams

Different

Different people, different faces,

different lands, different places.

Different background, different religions

Different ideas, different decisions.

Different names such as Brenda, Betty and Moniqué.

Different features make each of us unique.

Earth

Earth looks like it's made mostly of blue,

And it has a little green,

 it also has a touch of white which also can be seen.

Blue means water, white means clouds,

 green means lots of land.

I just wonder how it would feel, if the earth could fit inside my hand.

The Very Berry House

Once upon a time, there was a lady named Mrs. Cherry
She had a house made of all types of berries.
She had four children named after berries too!
Their names were Strawberry, Raspberry, Black Berry
and a berry named Blue.

Ice Cream Dreams

Stores

Different stores sell different things.

Some sell toys and some sell rings.

Some sell medicine and some sell cars.

Some even sell delicious candy bars.

Some stores sell fish that you can eat.

Some sell fruit and some sell meat.

If you need to buy something, you'll find it in a store.

Everything I told you is true, but you'll find so much more.

Safe

Safe is when you are cozy and warm.

Safe also means shelter from a storm.

Another meaning is feeling secure from any harm.

To me, "safe" means cuddling in my mother's arms.

Shining Rainbow

Every child, boy or girl
will shine around this glorious world.
Holding hands making this earth glow.
People of all different colors, shining like a beautiful rainbow.

Food For the Mind

Get comfortable under a tree of any kind.
Then get a book that interests you,
and start feeding your mind.

Teeth

Candy and cakes are tasty treats,

but they are not healthy snacks to eat.

It will rot your teeth if you eat too much cake and candy.

Take care of your teeth, because they will come in handy.

Your teeth are your very best friend.

If you treat them right, they'll be with you until the end.

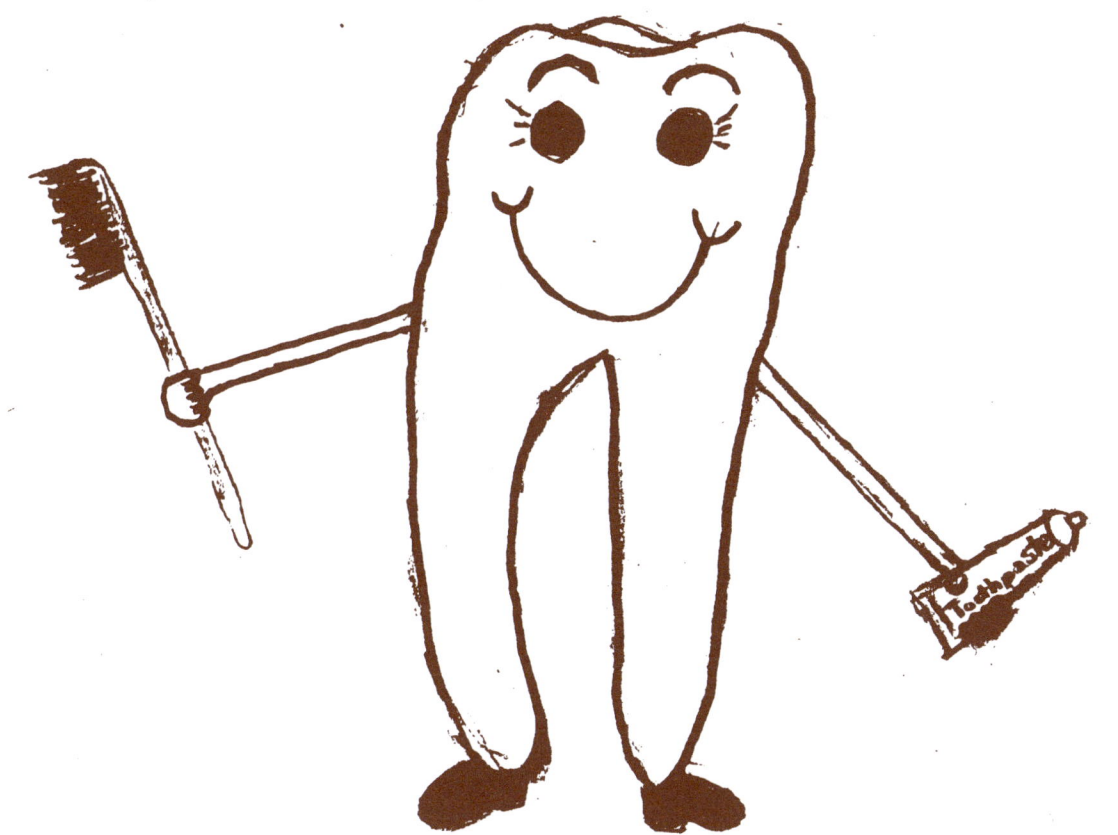

Time

Time has many meanings

Life and death are one

Time also means how long

It takes Earth to rotate the sun.

God gives every living creature a life span of how long they could live.

This is a precious gift, that only our heavenly Father can give.

Time is very mysterious, it goes by so fast.

When something happens right now, a minute later it's in the past!

Clouds

Clouds are white and they live in the sky.

You can see them well, because they're not very high.

I like to sit down on a nice sunny day,

to watch the clouds come, then watch them float away.

Not all clouds are the same, they are all different sizes,

and some have different names

Stratus is rainy, Cirrus is a fair day,

Cumulus clouds, there is no storm coming our way!

Ice Cream Dreams

Manners

In the morning or at night,
It's always good to be polite.
 No, it doesn't matter
who you're talking to,
You should always have manners
by saying "Please" and "Thank you!"

Your Neighbor

Everyone is your neighbor,

The nice ones and the ones who are mean.

Everyone is your neighbor,

The ones who are neat and the ones who aren't so clean.

Everyone is your neighbor, do you know the reason why?

God made us live under one blue sky.

God wants us to treat everyone the same.

We have nothing to lose and everything to gain.

Morning Passes

The birds chirp on my windowsill

while I lay in bed so quiet, so still.

I watch the sun rise through the warm clear glass.

I slowly notice that morning had passed.

Suddenly I Turned Around

Suddenly I turned around and she was gone!

This woman loved me from the first day I was born.

Suddenly I turned around and she was gone!

Though she isn't standing near me, her love will live on.

I am never alone, because grandma's spirit is with me.

I am sad that she is gone and happy that she is free.

One night grandma's spirit came to me, I felt peaceful and calm.

I saw something glowing in her hand. I asked her, "What's that in your palm?"

Grandma showed me a small globe, in her right hand.

I heard her whisper softly, "God is in command"!

A Special Pond

When I looked in a pond, what did I see,

I saw a simple reflection of me.

Then I looked closer and saw far beyond.....I saw a precious new world in this pond.

I saw little fishes swimming in my reflection,

I saw small crabs hiding in the sand for protection.

At first I just noticed my reflection but,

there was much more!

Just by looking in the pond's clear water

and on its sandy floor.

"The Messy Room"

What a messy room!

There's clothes everywhere, old broken rubber bands

and pieces of doll's hair.

On top of the dresser, there are old useless things.

There are old empty jars and lots of broken rings.

The wastebasket is filled to the top.

Oh no! she just stepped on a sticky lollipop!

Mother said, "Honey clean up that room!"

"But Ma" she said, "I can't find the broom!"

She finally cleaned her room until it shined.

Then the rest of her day worked out just fine.

Ice Cream Dreams

Violin

Violin is a pretty hard instrument to play.

It starts to get easy, if you practice everyday.

The first notes you should learn are G, D, A and E.

In the beginning, it was confusing and finally it became clear to me.

Did I mention on the violin,

there is a little place to rest your chin.

Bingo

Bingo is a game that's lots of fun to me.

Sometimes I play with friends or my family.

I like to play this game because it's not too hard.

All you have to do is pick out a lucky card.

We like to play this game over and over again.

It's simple, lots of fun and we like to see who'll win!

Ice Cream Dreams

Amazing Raindrops

When Mom or Dad is driving and it's raining outside,

All the raindrops big and small are going for a ride.

They're riding across the window, leaving their wet tracks.

They keep traveling forward and they never run back.

Some of them join together and some stay the way they are.

To me, the sparkling raindrops look like shooting stars.

Some of them look like they're having a race and some stick together.

They look so pure and harmless, but while driving, its really dangerous weather.

They tap against your window, like tap shoes on a smooth floor.

Raindrops are one type of precipitation, the whole world should adore.

Ice Cream Dreams

Avocado

I had an avocado, and I wanted to look inside.
The seed was really big and also very wide.
My mom cut it open for me, and I saw the lovely seed.
Then I said to myself, That's just what I need!"
I planted it and watched it grow, weed by weed.
I remember when it started from just a lovely seed.

Ice Cream Dreams

Book, Books, Books

History books, coloring books
Books about pirates, cowboys and crooks.
Books about Kings, Queens and Knights.
There's even books about equal rights.
There are scary books that might give you a fright.
So let's read a good book tonight!

Colors

Gold is the color of the sun, so beautiful and bright.
White is the color of the stars, glimmering in the dark night.

Green is the color of grass, sparkling with morning dew.
The sky is a magnificent color of a beautiful powder **blue**.

Brown is the color in the middle of the tree, which is called a bark.
Black is a beautiful color that is peaceful and dark.

Gray is the color of some clouds, when rain is about to appear.
When you feel sad and need to cry, your tears are salty and clear.

Colors make the world a beautiful place to live.
Every presence on and around this earth has a different color to give!

Ice Cream Dreams

Smiley Town

I would like to tell you about a rather unique place.

It is where you could only wear a smile upon your face.

In this place, no one's sad and no one has a frown.

The place is called Happy Place

and the town is called Smiley Town.

Everyone walks around whistling a happy tune.

They walk around smiling from morning until noon.

Smiley town is a very comforting place and it's lots of fun!

There is no violence, no knives and no types of guns.

There are no drugs, cigarettes or cigars.

The air is not polluted with smoke from trucks or cars.

The water is crystal clear and taste so pure.

This unpolluted water knows how to cure.

It can cure cancer and it can cure the common cold.

To be cured by this magical water,

it doesn't matter if you're young or old.

When I took a good look at the water, the water wore a smile too!

Like I said, Smiley Town is a unique place,

Even the water and sky can't be blue!

Squirrel

I saw a squirrel climb up a tree.
Sometimes that squirrel just stared at me.

When I walked toward him, he ran away.
I wondered why he didn't want to stay.

Squirrels are cute as can be, but don't bother them because they want to run free!

Ice Cream Dreams

Lady Liberty

Lady Liberty stands proud and tall.

Lady Liberty stands for peace and freedom to us all,

Immigrants are welcome to the land of the free.

I'm glad you made your first stop at the Statue of Liberty.

Lady Liberty is truly a great sight.

Her torch glows during the day, and all through the night.

The Rock

I saw a little grayish rock lying on the ground,

I said hi! to that rock, but it didn't make a sound.

I wonder if that rock was feeling shy,

or if that rock just didn't want to say hi.

Finally my mom said, that rock can't talk!

That rock can't eat and that rock can't walk!

That rock can't do things like we can do.

That rock has no feelings unlike me and you.

Starfish

Starfish have arms called rays, tube feet and a mouth on their underside.
Some are one to 65 centimeters wide.
Starfish belong to a family of Echinoderms.
They eat clams, mussels, oysters, sponges and worms.
Their rough and leathery skin usually grows a spine.
Starfish lay their eggs mostly in the springtime.
Baby starfish are called larva, and grow everything they need to stay alive.
Life without all their important parts, they wouldn't be able to survive.

"Mother Bird"

Mother bird said; "my babies open your mouth wide,

I want to put something yummy and tasty inside.

It will wiggle and it will squirm,

it is a nice big juicy worm."

Ice Cream Dreams

Wouldn't it be great if.......

Wouldn't it be great if everyone could love one another.

Wouldn't it be great if everyone treated you like a brother.

Wouldn't it be great if all of us could get along.

Wouldn't it be great if we were that strong.

Wouldn't it be great if no one was ever poor.

Wouldn't it be great if no one suffered anymore!

Yes! It would be great!

CHICKEN

Mmmmmm! Chicken wings, chicken breasts.

I like chicken legs the best.

Chicken that's baked, chicken that's fried,

Chicken with potatoes or onions on the side!

Cookies and Tea

I bought some cookies to go with my tea,

enough for you and enough for me.

I'll put them all on top of the plate.

We have 1, 2, 3, 4, 5, 6, 7, 8.

We'll split the 8 cookies 4 by 4, if we eat them all,

There would be no more!

Ice Cream Dreams

Anything is Possible

Anything is possible, here's the reason why.

You've heard of a laughing hyena, but have you ever seen one cry?

Anything is possible, a mouse chasing a cat.

A dog going to a party, wearing a purple hat.

Anything is possible, a tree eating its fruit,

A tiger without a tail, a bear playing a flute.

Anything is possible, a gold and silver sky.

A train that runs on dirt, a crow that doesn't fly.

Anything is possible, a flag with no design,

A flower with no leaves, a pine tree with no pines.

Anything is possible, if you use your mind.

You just need a good imagination and let your thoughts unwind!

Ice Cream Dreams

THE MARCHING SOLDIERS

There once were many soldiers who stood shoulder to shoulder.

Some were very young, and some were much, much older.

They marched around cities as well as states.

The total of soldiers in each troop was nine hundred and twenty-eight

The soldiers marched for love, peace and grace.

The soldiers stood side by side, it didn't matter what race.

The soldiers believed it was great to give,

and hate in your heart was the wrong way to live.

Teddy

Sit down, relax and get ready!
I want to tell you about a special hamster name Teddy.

My sister has a hamster that is so cute and it doesn't bite.
Sometimes we can hear Teddy running on her squeaky wheel at night.

When she gets hungry, we give her lettuce and carrots to eat.
Sometimes we also give her a piece of hot dog as a treat.

Teddy lays out flat when she feels too warm
and she rolls up in a ball when she's cold.
The entire family loves Teddy a lot and she's only two years old.

This poem must come to an end,
now that you've heard about our special family friend!

Things Come and Go

The petal of a tulip

The smell of a rose

These are things that come and go.

A gentle snowflake tickling my nose.

The warm sand rubbing between my toes

These are things that come and go.

The way the wind blows and blows

These are things that come and go.

All of these things are a part of natures flow

All of these things come and go.

Ice Cream Dreams

We're Different

We are all different, not one of us are the same.

All of us have different fingerprints as well as different names.

All of us have different hobbies and different things we like to do.

I am proud of who I am, and you should be proud of you!

My Secret Hiding Place

I have a little secret space.

A small quiet hiding place.

It's not much room, so only one person can fit.

There's only one tiny stool for one person to sit.

Hope

If you want to do something,
    dreaming is just one part.
You'll also need to keep practicing
    and do it from your heart.

If someone says you'll never be somebody,
    just continue to walk with pride.
No matter what people say or do,
    they can't take the hope you have inside!

Amazing Sun

I would like to tell you about our amazing sun.

It is a bright star that gives light to everyone.

The sun is 864,000 miles wide.

You can fit more than one million Earths inside.

The sun is a very hot ball of gas.

We know the sun is half way through its life.

But we're not sure how much longer it will last.

Koalas

A Koala is a cute marsupial,
with a pouch soft and gray.
Koalas are active on trees all during the day.

Koalas are excellent climbers
and they live on Eucalyptus trees.
Part of a koala diet, is to eat certain Eucalyptus leaves.

Koalas can only eat certain leaves,
because some are filled with toxic waste.
Koalas smell the leaves to makes sure they're good,
before they try a taste.

Koalas are vegetarians, they never ever eat meat.
Koalas rarely go to a river, because they get water from the leaves they eat.

When a baby koala is grown,
it will find Eucalyptus leaves on its own.

Once in a while a Koala might,
come visit its mom and spend a night.

Koala

A **Koala** is furry

A **Koala** is cute

A **Koala** likes to climb trees,

but not as much as monkeys do!

COURTNEY GRIMES
Brittney's Younger Sister

"School Supplies"

A ruler is used for measuring things.

How small is an ant and how long is an eagle's wings!

A scissors is used to cut things.

Can you cut this paper or trim my strings?

A pencil is used to write, draw and trace.

Would you draw a bright smile on my face?

Paper is used to write on top of.

Can you write your name and write the word love?

The Café

A young gentleman went to a café
to drink some coffee with a young lady named May.
They asked for more coffee to keep their bodies nice and warm,
because it is winter and there is a terrible snowstorm!

Turkey

Here's a turkey having lots of fun,

until a man comes with a big shot gun.

Bang! Bang! That's how we get it on Thanksgiving Day.

Poor little turkey, some people say!

The Girl Who Loved to Read

There once was a little girl,

who loved to read books everyday.

She read so much, she hardly had time to play.

She liked all kinds of books,

she even liked books that rhyme.

She also like reading books that took her back in time.

Thunder and Lightning

Sometimes, do you ever wonder

how far lightning travels and how loud is thunder?

Do you believe God is bowling in the sky,

whenever you hear thunder way up high?

Whenever you see the flash of lightning.

In your opinion, is it scary and frightening?

Lightning is just a bright flash of light between two clouds.

Thunder is just a rumbling noise, which is very, very loud.

The Gift

I love to write poetry,
it's lots of fun.
It's a special gift, God gave me
to share with everyone!

NOTE FROM THE AUTHOR.

"When I grow up, I want to continue writing. I hope everyone enjoys reading my book. Anything you dream can come true! Never be afraid to dream! I've only begun to dream."

ABOUT THE AUTHOR

Brittney Moniqué Grimes was born on August 28, 1989, in Queens, New York. The second of three children born to Mr. & Mrs. Grimes. She resides in Baldwin, New York with her parents and sisters, Tiffany and Courtney.

Brittney attended the Edward Hart Elementary School in Flushing, Queens, and Shubert Elementary School in Baldwin. She is now attending Middle School.

Brittney started reading poetry at the age of four and started writing poetry at the age of six. At seven years of age, she won several awards for her poetry. At the tender age of 8, Brittney published her first book, *Poetry For A Child By A Child*. At the age of 10, she published her second book entitled *Poetry For A Child By A Child Workbook*. At the young age of 11, she has published her third book entitled *Ice Cream Dreams*.

Brittney appeared on the television stage of the World Famous Apollo Theatre and received a standing ovation after reciting her poem **"Children Of The World."** She has also appeared on different local news programs. She recites her poetry for churches, schools, libraries, nursing homes and universities. Some of her poetry has appeared in newspapers, magazines and additional poetry books.